THE REFRIGERATOR DOOR GALLERY

MacGregor

CARTOONS
- from the -
NEWS-PRESS

Published by
MacTOONS
Fort Myers. FL

Library of Congress Catalog Card Number: 96-94812
ISBN: 0-9654843-0-0

Printed in the U.S. by Newspaper Printing Company, Tampa, FL.

Thanks to: Ernie Foxworth, Steve Olive, JoAnn Kelso, the production staff of the News-Press, Garth Francis and Ken Gooderham.

Special thanks to Barbara Havens for her undying patience and encouragement...

PORTER GOSS
14TH DISTRICT, FLORIDA

108 CANNON BUILDING
WASHINGTON, DC 20515-0913
(202) 225-2536

COMMITTEES:
RULES
CHAIRMAN, SUBCOMMITTEE
ON LEGISLATIVE AND BUDGET PROCESS

PERMANENT SELECT COMMITTEE
ON INTELLIGENCE
STANDARDS OF OFFICIAL CONDUCT

DISTRICT OFFICES:
2000 MAIN STREET
SUITE 303
FT. MYERS, FL 33901
(941) 332-4677

3301 TAMIAMI TRAIL EAST
BUILDING F, SUITE 212
NAPLES, FL 33962
(941) 774-8060

PUNTA GORDA
(941) 639-0051

Congress of the United States
House of Representatives
Washington, DC 20515—0914

Dear Cartoon Gourmets,

As in countless other homes, in my house the refrigerator is the center of the universe -- and the refrigerator door serves not only as the gateway to refreshment and nourishment -- it is a family message center, command post and showcase of great thought, pursuit, and accomplishment.

Competition for space is tough -- lots of family activity these days! But Doug MacGregor is there -- represented by one of his current zingers or perhaps by an older, but timeless truth he captured especially well with his pen and ink. He hits the funny bone or pokes incisively at an issue we have been stirring up around the kitchen table.

Humorist Will Rogers once said that he doesn't know jokes, he just watches the government and reports the facts. Doug MacGregor watches us all and reports the facts through cartoons that make us laugh.

He serves up political life in delectable slices. Few issues or public figures in Southwest Florida in the past decade have missed Doug's menu. His presentation is always memorable, always one of a kind.

As The Refrigerator Door Gallery clearly shows, Doug isn't shy about those tough recipes. He's tackled the trickiest subjects -- even those involving the President of the United States.

If the most recent election season has whetted your appetite for a lighter diet of political fare, this book is for you. Save space on your refrigerator door.

Happy reading,

Porter Goss

P.S. Celebrated political cartoonist J.N. "Ding" Darling was active in Southwest Florida in wildlife conservation. His work led to the Duck Stamp Program. Could it be that The Refrigerator Door Gallery will lead to a new "food stamp program" in honor of Doug MacGregor?

The Author...

It is said a picture is worth a thousand words. If that is true, *News-Press* editorial cartoonist Doug MacGregor has generated more than a million words of commentary. Whether it's roasting Congress over pork-barrel legislation, grinding lawmakers in Tallahassee over partisan gridlock, or criticizing county commissioners for caving into special interests, Doug has covered it!

For sixteen years he has been creating five editorial cartoons a week. Four thousand cartoons later you can still find him inking away at his drawing board meeting deadline for the next day's paper.

A 1979 graduate of Syracuse University, Doug began his career drawing sports cartoons for the *Daily Orange*. In 1980 he moved to eastern Connecticut and became editorial cartoonist and graphics illustrator for the *Norwich Bulletin*. For eight years he drew for all sections of the newspaper, but was best known for his caustic cartoons on the editorial page. His first book, <u>Collection of MacGregor Editorial Cartoons from the Norwich Bulletin</u> was published in 1988. Doug could also be seen in *USA Today* from 1985-1990 drawing occasional guest cartoons for the editorial page.

In 1982, a cartoon Doug drew about Ronald Reagan was selected for the cover of the annual book, <u>Best Editorial Cartoons of the Year.</u> In the winter of 1987, while visiting his parents in Port Charlotte, Doug applied for a job at the News-Press in Fort Myers. His chance to thaw out his drawing hand came to pass the following year when a position opened up in the News-Press Graphics Department. He has been drawing daily editorial cartoons including his popular "MacGregor's Boulevard" on Sundays ever since.

Doug self-syndicates his work to several newspapers throughout the "Sunshine State". He also gets out from behind the drawing board regularly visiting area classrooms to spread the message about keeping up on current events by reading the daily newspaper.

He has won awards in Connecticut (*Eduction Association Media Award, 1982*) and Florida (*School Boards Association Media Award, 1992 and FTP/NEA Newsmaker Award, 1993*) for his volunteer work at local schools. A member of the *American Association of Editorial Cartoonists* and the *National Cartoonist Society*. MacGregor also has won several national and statewide cartooning awards. Most recently he became an eight-time national *Best of Gannett* winner and two-time *Florida Press Club Award* recipient for his editorial cartoons. He was also a recipient of the *Society of Professional Journalists Sunshine State Award* for Editorial Cartoons in 1994.

Doug lives in Fort Myers. When he is not drawing cartoons, he is out playing golf looking for more cartoon ideas.

MAIN MENU

 **National & International Appetizers**
7 - 59

 **MacGregor's Boulevard**
Color **145 - 160**
B & W **161 - 175**

 **State Snacks**
60 - 111

 **Sports Samplers**
176 - 187

 **Local Entrees**
112 - 143

 **After Dinner Conversation Peaces**
188 - 192

"Humorist Will Rogers once said that he doesn't know jokes, he just watches the government and reports the facts. Doug MacGregor watches us all and reports the facts through cartoons that make us laugh...

As _The Refrigerator Door Gallery_ clearly shows, Doug isn't shy about those tough recipes. He's tackled some of the trickiest subjects -- even those involving the President of the United States."

-Congressman Porter Goss

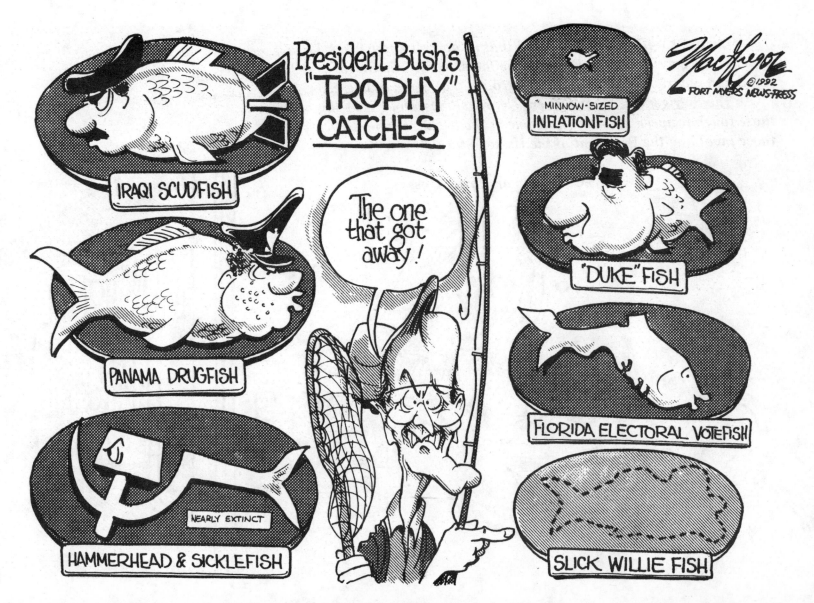

POLITICAL PROMISES

CAP'T CLINTON

POLITICAL COMPROMISES

NEWS-PRESS AT FORT MYERS ©1993

13

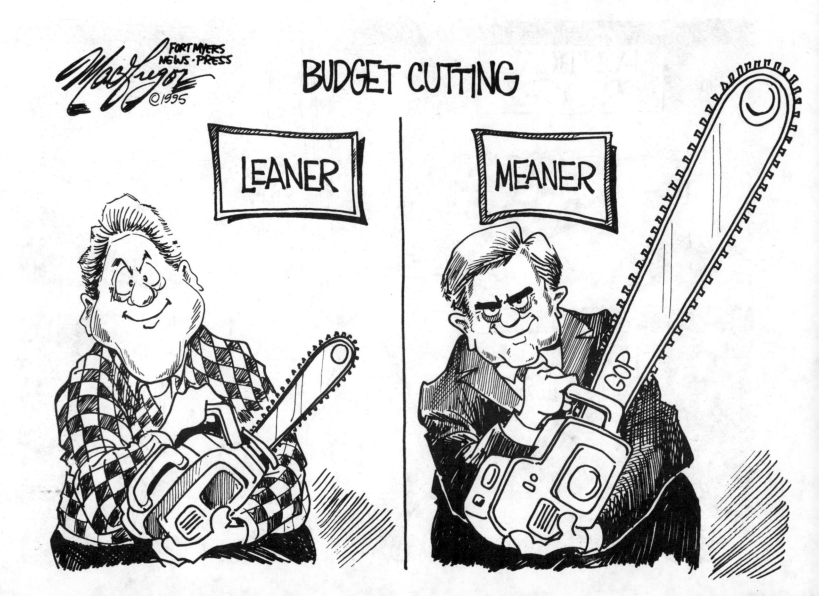

BUDGET CUTTING

LEANER   MEANER

15

WATERGATE
1974

WHITEWATER
1996

FORT MYERS
NEWS-PRESS

18

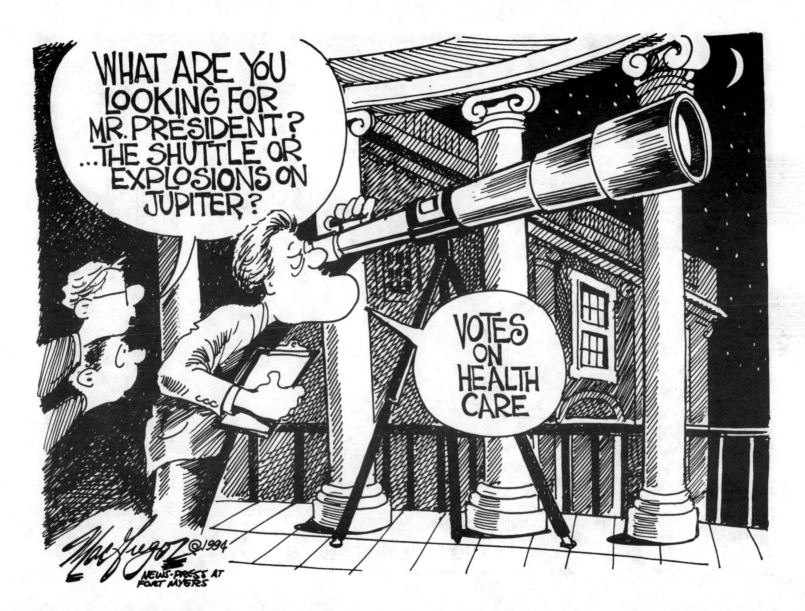

19

20

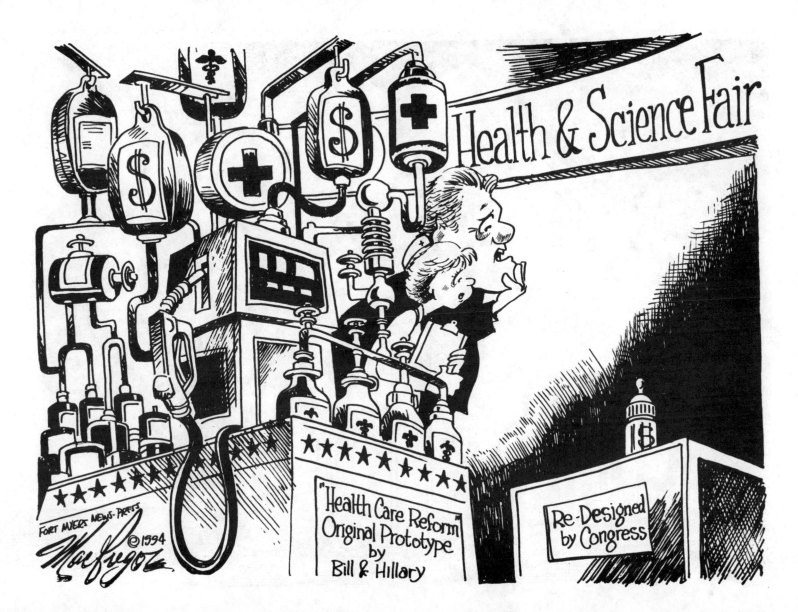

"I can not tell a lie, I chopped down a few campaign promises"

GEORGE WASHINGTON CLINTON

NEWS-PRESS
MacHugh ©1993

"The only thing we have to fear is the the cost of health care"

FRANKLIN DELANO CLINTON

☆ PRESIDENTIAL PROFILES ☆

"Ask not what your country can do for you, but what you can do to *sacrifice*"

JOHN FITZGERALD CLINTON

"I want you and a few more of your tax dollars"

UNCLE BILL

26

29

31

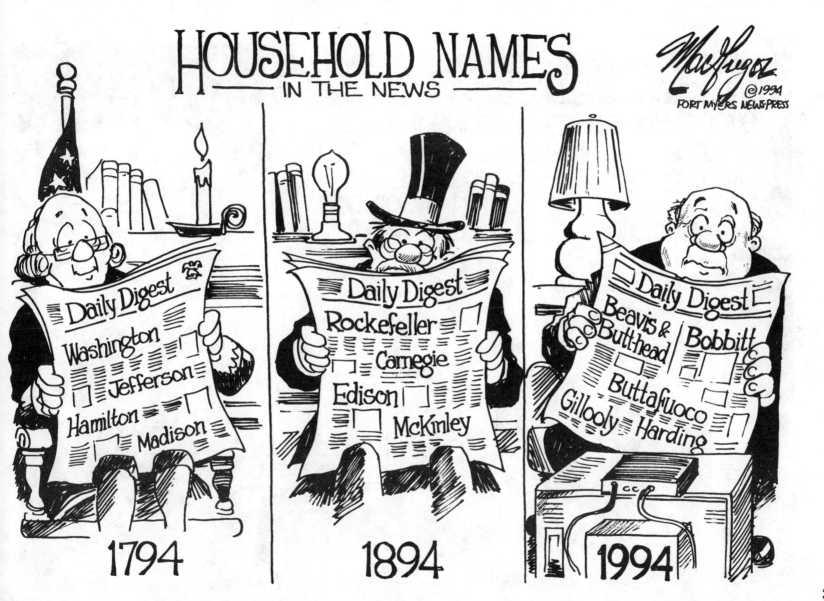

34

35

Sultan of Swat

"HEY, COULD YOU PIPE DOWN BACK THERE? I'M TRYING TO READ, IF YOU DON'T MIND"

Peacekeeping in Mogadishu

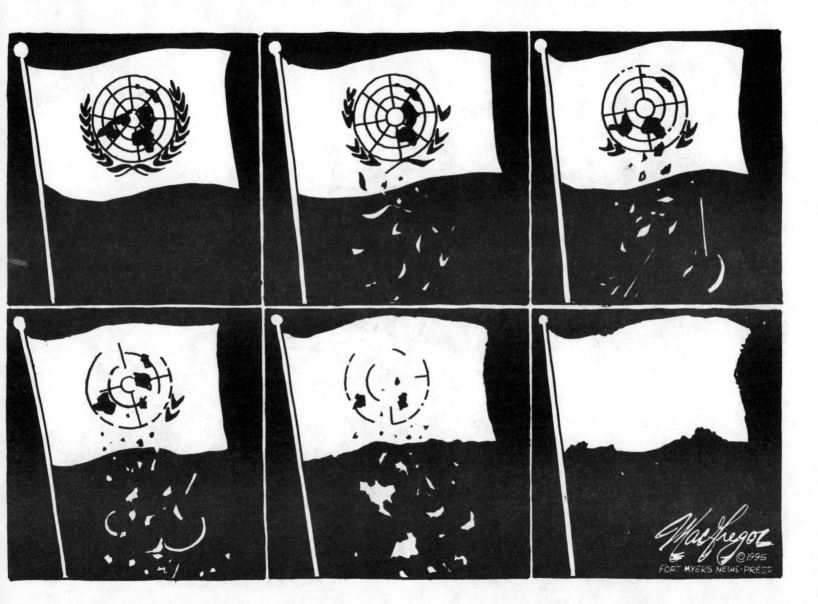

41

CATCHING EACH OTHER'S DRIFT

STATE OF THE UNION PARKING LOT

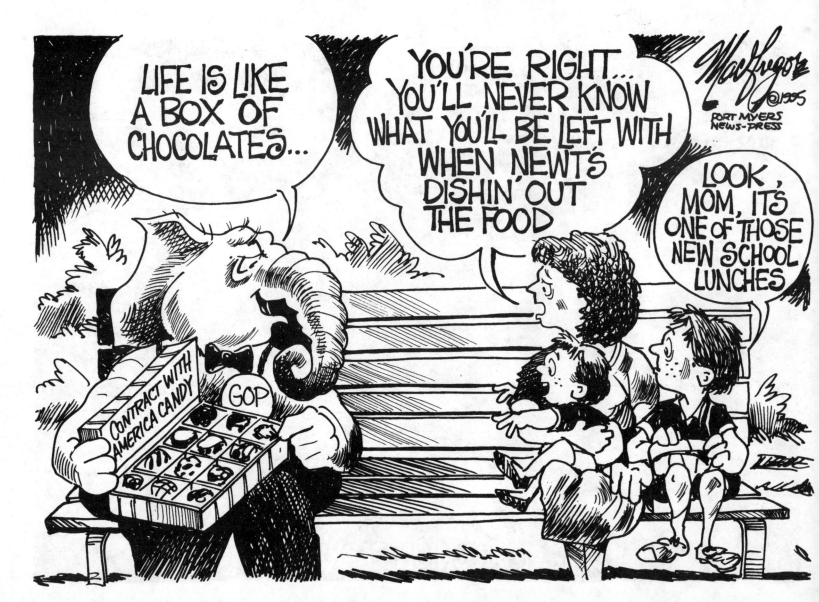

44

ESSENTIAL WORKER

NON-ESSENTIAL

46

48

CAPITOL HILL RAIN FOREST

SENATE Kissing Booth

Out of Business

TAKE A NUMBER
95

PACKWOOD

FORT MYERS ©1995
NEWS-PRESS
MacGregor

'82 '82 '92 '91 '93

51

CAPITOL HILL FLOOR PLAN

A. ROTUNDA
B. HOSPITAL LOBBY
C. DOCTOR'S LOBBY
D. BIG SUGAR LOBBY
E. FARM LOBBY
F. TOBACCO LOBBY
G. OIL LOBBY
H. GAS LOBBY
I. THIS LOBBY SPACE FOR SALE
J. Q. PUBLIC LOBBY

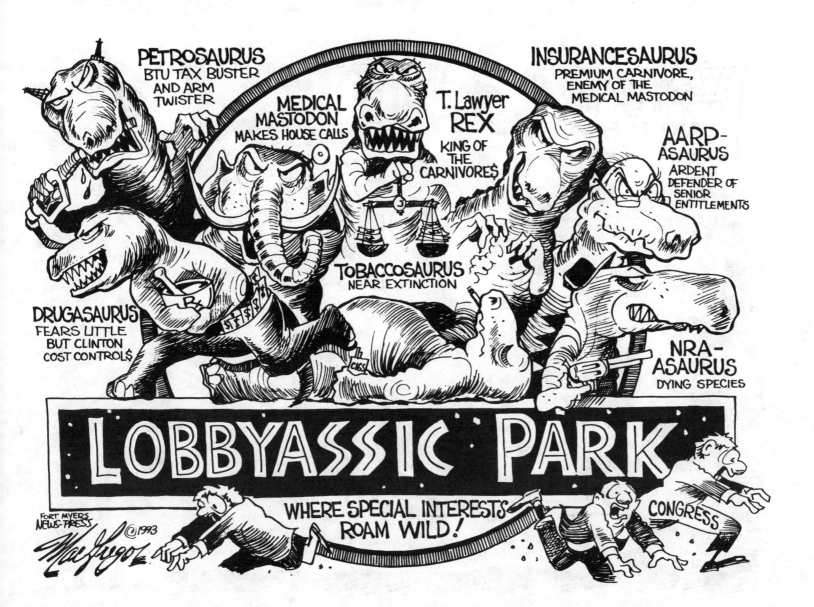

54

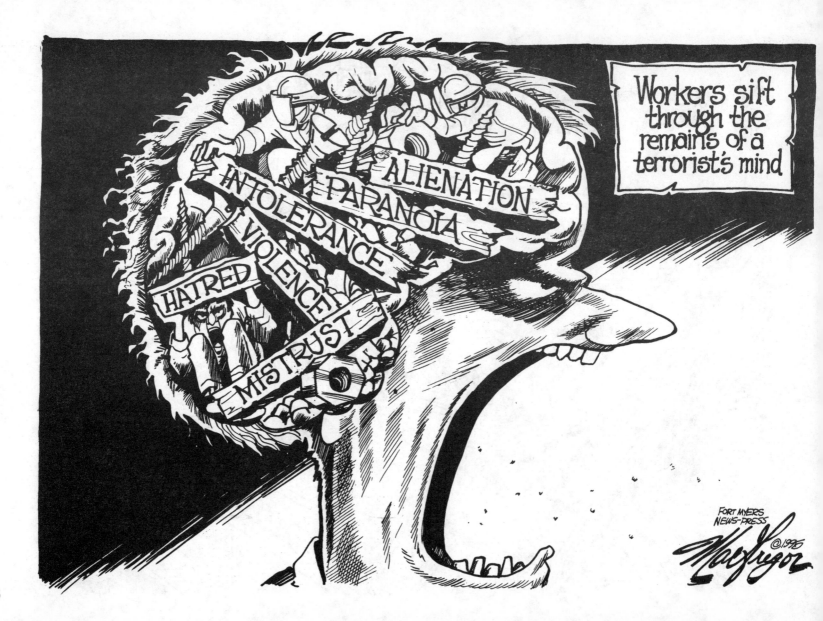

HAMAS

NEWS-PRESS AT
FORT MYERS

© 1996
MacGregor

57

The Long Climb Over Apartheid...

BALLOT BOX

"I can't think of an editorial cartoonist more qualified in his field or whom I have more enjoyed, than Doug MacGregor and his collection of works, _The Refrigerator Door Gallery._ Irreverent and always on target, Doug's cartoons poke gentle fun at various government issues, whether national, statewide or local in scope. I, too, have been the brunt of many of his creative 'toons and always enjoy his humor. I also appreciate his apparent cynicism, particularly after being an observer of government for the last 14 years, Doug's insightful cartoons are a significant mix of zing and humor and, with this new book, readers - and viewers are offered a refreshing change of pace."

-State Representative J. Keith Arnold

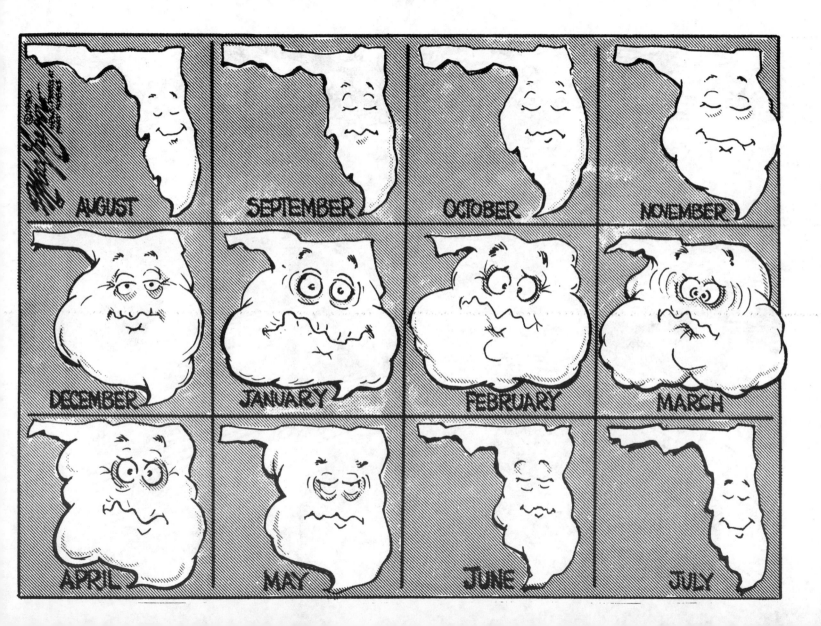

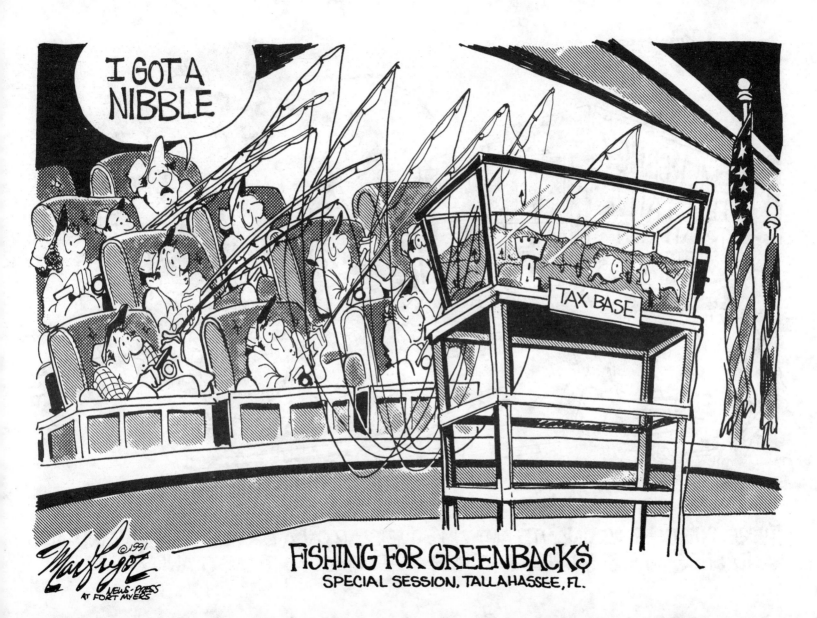

FISHING FOR GREENBACKS
SPECIAL SESSION, TALLAHASSEE, FL.

"THERE SHE GOES AGAIN... IT'S AMAZING, WE SLAP ON A COUPLE OF NEW BAND-AIDS AND SHE'S OFF SURVIVING ANOTHER YEAR OF CUTS, BUMPS AND BRUISES."

Sacred Cows

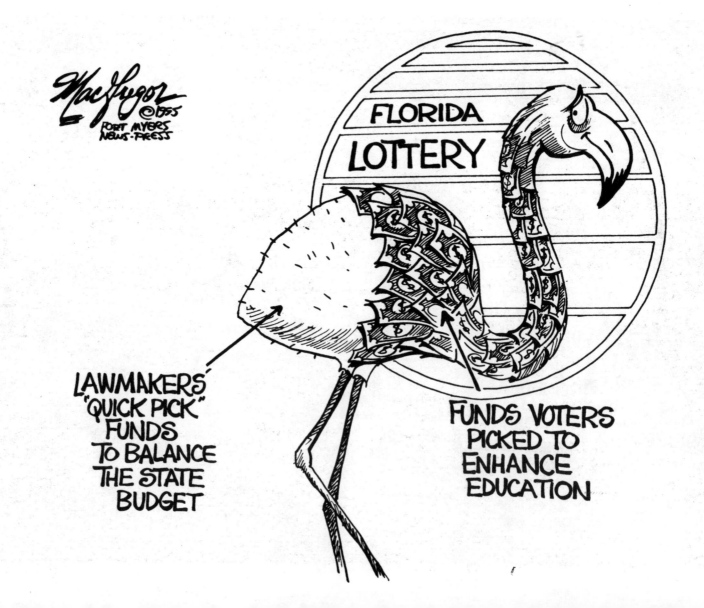

"O.K. EVERYBODY TAKE ANOTHER DEEP BREATH AND HOLD IT,
WE HAVE FIVE MORE STUDENTS COMING INTO OUR CLASS."

TALLAHASSEE CONTROL

NEEDED LOCAL CONTROL

73

If a man empties his purse into his head, no man can take it away from him.
An investment in knowledge always pays the best interest.

-Benjamin Franklin

TALLAHASSEE AGENDA CHOIR

**ANOTHER FLORIDA
RESIDENT MURDERED**

**ANOTHER FLORIDA
TOURIST MURDERED**

85

There once was a governor who lived in a shoe,
He had so many immigrants he knew what he had to do.
He gave them welfare, health care and books.
He cared for the helpless. He locked up the crooks.

But, all this cost money, so much in fact,
That he pleaded to Congress to get into the act.
"Enough is enough," the governor said,
"Help me pay these bills, or I'll sue the Fed."

88

89

90

NEWS-PRESS AT
FORT MYERS
© 1992

ABSTRACT EXPRESSIONISM

CUBISM

REAPPORTIONMENT

91

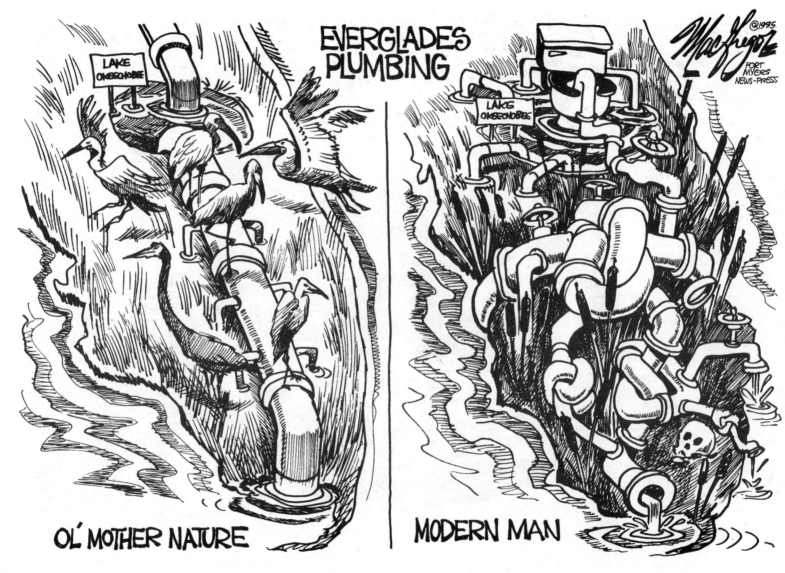

98

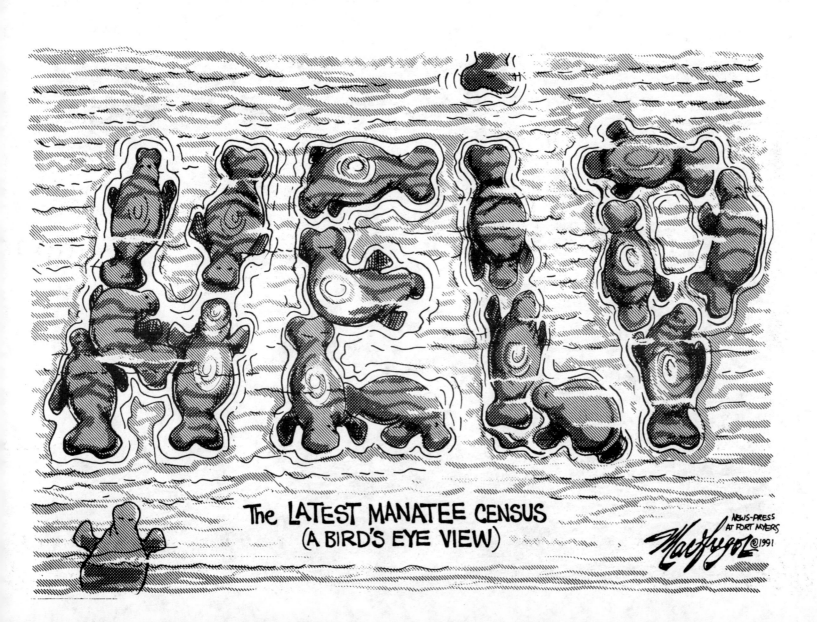

The LATEST MANATEE CENSUS
(A BIRD'S EYE VIEW)

99

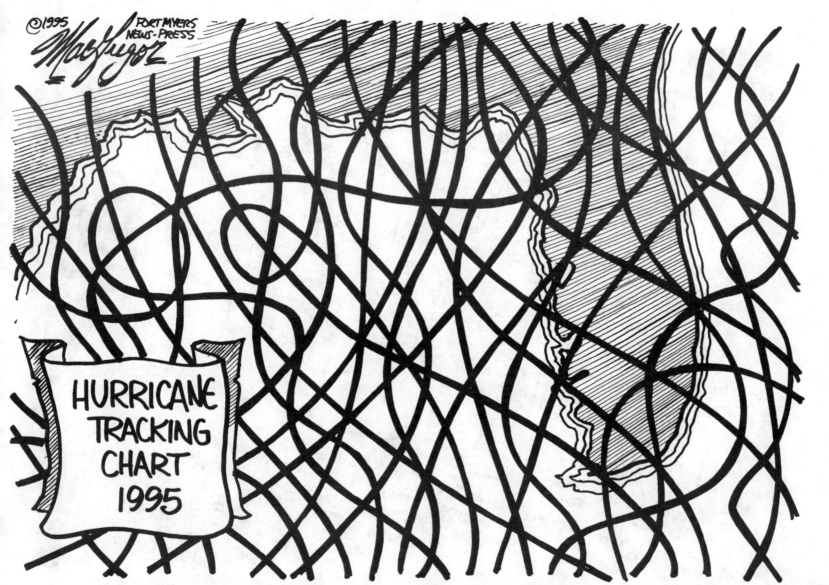

WHAT TO PACK WHEN COMING TO FLORIDA

FISHING POLES   BEACH WEAR   CAMERAS   GOLF CLUBS   PLEASURE CRAFT   BEACH UMBRELLA   BEACH SAND

MacGregor ©1995
FORT MYERS NEWS-PRESS

NORTHERN POLAR SEASON

©1991
NEWS-PRESS AT FORT MYERS

FLORIDA SOLAR SEASON

NORTHERN PINE	FLORIDA PALM
PARTRIDGE	PELICAN
MISTLETOE	BROMELIADS
STOCKINGS HUNG FROM THE MANTEL	STOCKINGS HUNG FROM THE WET BAR
BRICK FIREPLACE	GAS GRILL
WOOD FOR THE FIRE	BRIQUETS FOR THE BAR-B-Q
CHESTNUTS ROASTING ON AN OPEN FIRE	JUMBO SHRIMP GRILLING ON AN OPEN FIRE
SNOWPLOW	LAWN MOWER
HOT TODDY	FROZEN MARGARITA
PUMPKIN PIE	KEY LIME PIE
ICE SKATES	ROLLERBLADES
LONG JOHNS	SHORT SHORTS
FLANNEL SHIRT	FLOWERED SHIRT
SHOVEL	SAND WEDGE

"Without question, Doug MacGregor is the most respected journalist in Southwest Florida. His beautifully illustrated, yet razor-sharp political satire depicted in his acutely relevant political cartoons make him unique in today's print world. He has the ability to cut you deep with a swift stroke of his pencil or pen, yet one never needs stitches because the cuts somehow quickly and magically heal. Doug has that one-of-a-kind ability to tell the truth, no matter how painful...It's obvious he loves his work, the profession and, best of all, people. Those who possess this book will have a treasure ..."

-Fort Myers Mayor Wilbur C. Smith III

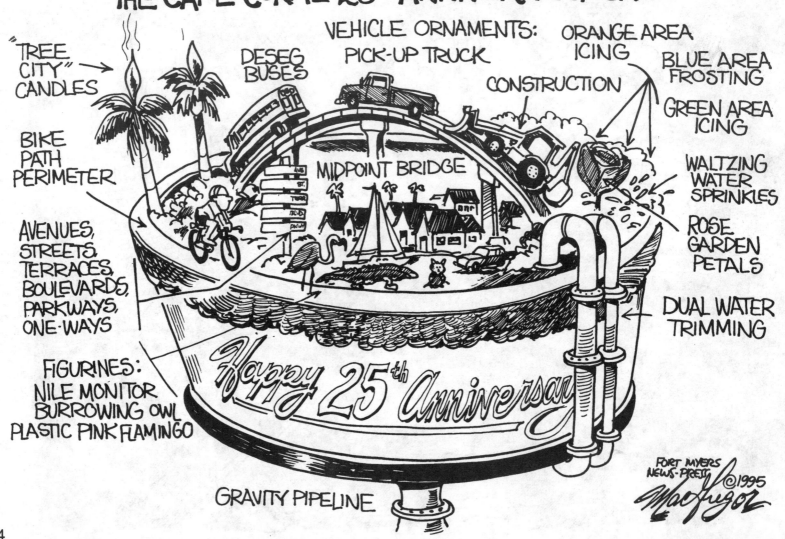

THE CAPE CORAL 25TH ANNIVERSARY CAKE

VEHICLE ORNAMENTS:
PICK-UP TRUCK

ORANGE AREA ICING

"TREE CITY" CANDLES

DESEG BUSES

CONSTRUCTION

BLUE AREA FROSTING

GREEN AREA ICING

BIKE PATH PERIMETER

MIDPOINT BRIDGE

WALTZING WATER SPRINKLES

AVENUES, STREETS, TERRACES, BOULEVARDS, PARKWAYS, ONE-WAYS

ROSE GARDEN PETALS

DUAL WATER TRIMMING

FIGURINES:
NILE MONITOR
BURROWING OWL
PLASTIC PINK FLAMINGO

Happy 25th Anniversary

FORT MYERS NEWS-PRESS ©1995

GRAVITY PIPELINE

114

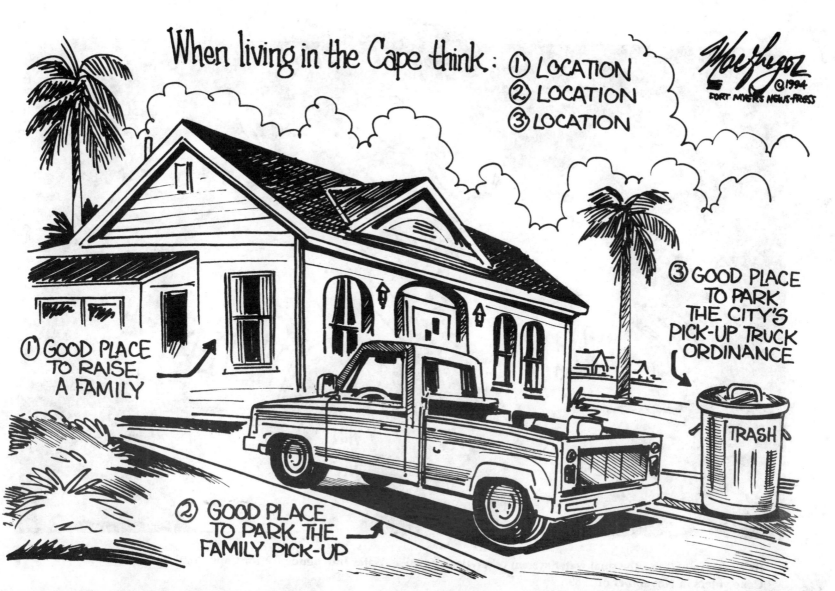

By a margin of 2 to 1 the dual water system otherwise known as Water Independence for Cape Coral (WICC) is approved by Cape voters in November of 1989.

CALLING THE SHOT

121

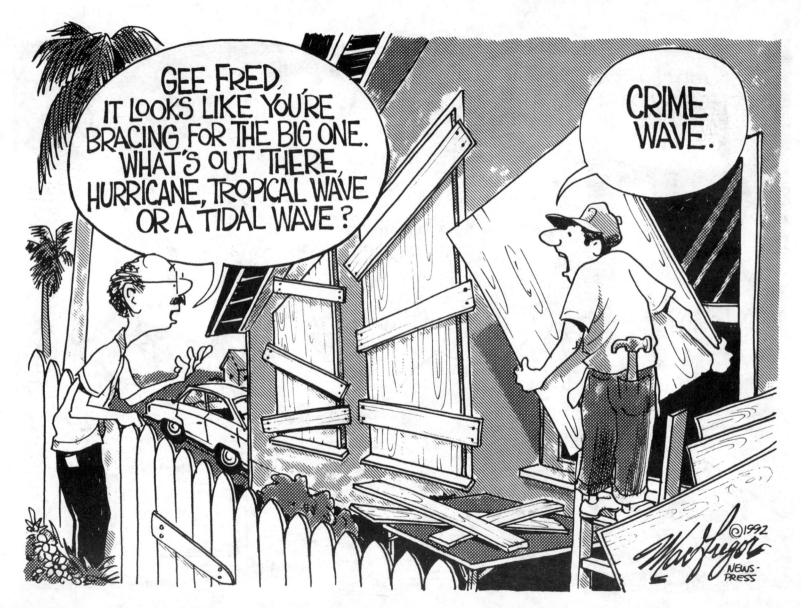

FORT MYERS
NEWS-PRESS
© 1996

THE SCHOOL BOARD OF LEE COUNTY

Old

THE CHRISTIAN COALITION SCHOOL BOARD OF LEE COUNTY

Bible

POLITICAL VERSION

New

125

126

IF FGCU FOES HAD BEEN AROUND IN CENTURIES PAST...

MacGregor ©1995
FORT MYERS NEWS-PRESS

GOD WOULD HAVE BEEN READING PETITIONS ON THE SEVENTH DAY, NOT RESTING

NOAH WOULD HAVE NEEDED WATER DISTRICT PERMITS TO FLOAT

THE GREAT PYRAMID WOULD HAVE BEEN A TRAPEZOID

ROME WOULD NOT HAVE BEEN BUILT IN ONE DAY, A WEEK, A YEAR, OR EVEN A MILLENNIUM FOR THAT MATTER

MOUNT RUSHMORE WOULD BE HEADLESS

THERE WOULD BE NO LIGHT AT THE END OF THE CHUNNEL

AFTER EIGHTEEN YEARS OF DELIBERATION, MITIGATION, LITIGATION AND MULTITUDINOUS DELAYS, FGCU FINALLY OPENS ITS DOORS AND CHANGES ITS NAME...

IF DA VINCI HAD GONE TO SCHOOL WITH A SIX PERIOD DAY

Dr. James Adams
1936 ~ 1994

In a surprise move, Lee County administrator Marsha Segal-George submits her conditional resignation two days before commissioners St. Cerny, Lopez-Wolfe and Slisher plan to fire her in June, 1991.

In one week, Lee County administrator Segal-George and deputy administrator Frank Nocera resign. County commissioners John Manning and Ray Judah also step down from their chairman and vice chairman positions.

After reading an emotional resignation statement, Vicki Lopez-Wolfe bolts from the Lee County commission chambers on Jan. 27, 1993.

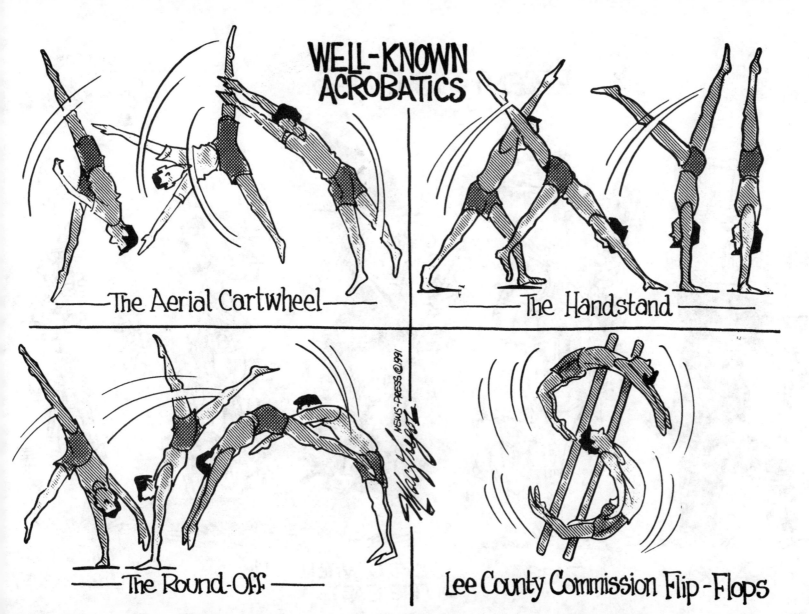

WELL-KNOWN ACROBATICS

The Aerial Cartwheel

The Handstand

The Round-Off

Lee County Commission Flip-Flops

137

RECENT SIGHTINGS...

FRANK   ELVIS   WICKED WITCH OF THE EAST   HOUDINI   BUDGET of LEE COUNTY

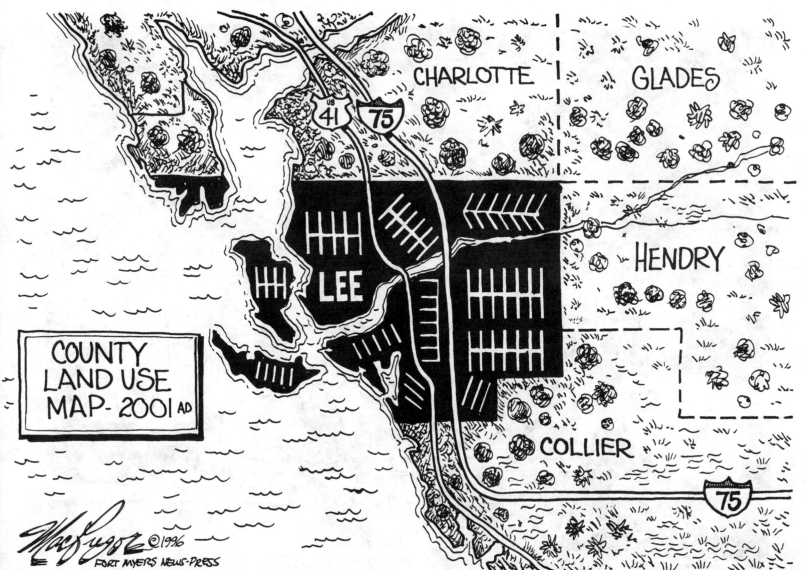

COUNTY LAND USE MAP- 2001 AD

CHARLOTTE

GLADES

LEE

HENDRY

COLLIER

MacNelly ©1996
FORT MYERS NEWS-PRESS

139

Lee County Sheriff McDougall asks for an 18 percent increase in his budget for 1993-1994. With Lee County commissioners only willing to give him a 5 percent increase, McDougall takes his appeal on a road trip to the Florida Cabinet in Tallahassee.

143

THE HOUSE THAT WILBUR BUILT (QUICKLY)

Lee County Sheriff McDougall gets a hefty $5 million, 18 percent budget increase from county commissioners in 1991.

152

In May of 1992 the Lee County School District became the first school system in the country to allow HIV testing at high school health fairs. School board members later rescinded the program in a controversial vote on August 8, 1995.

155

MAKING WAVES...

Cape Coral city councilman Gary Giebels and his six-item November 1991 ballot referendum battle against Mayor Joe Mazurkiewicz and the Cape's status quo. All six ballot items failed at the polls.

EXTENDING A HAND FROM SOUTHWEST FLORIDA THANKS TO YOU...

After Hurricane Andrew, Southwest Floridians open their hearts and their pocketbooks to help South Floridian victims.

Governorship.

Presidency.

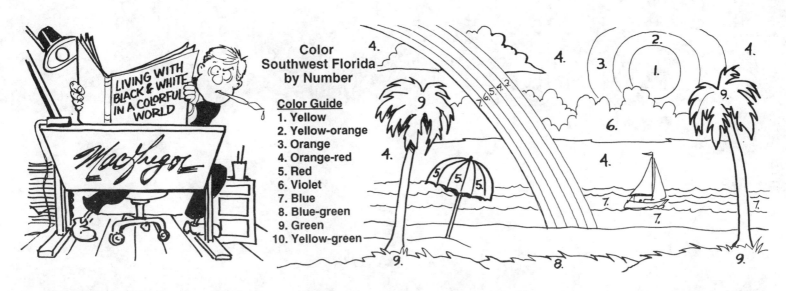

Much to the chagrin of the artist and his readers, *MacGregor's Boulevard* is moved to the bottom of the second page of the Sunday Insight section in black and white on September 19, 1993.

162

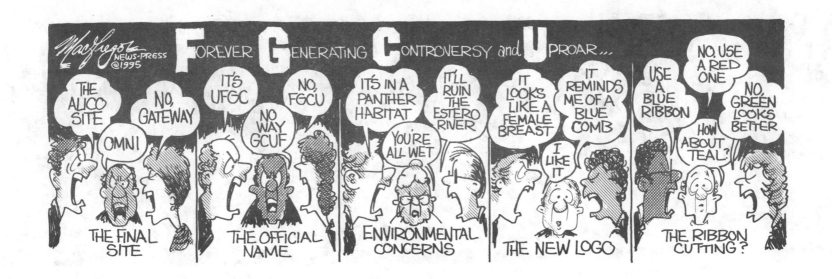

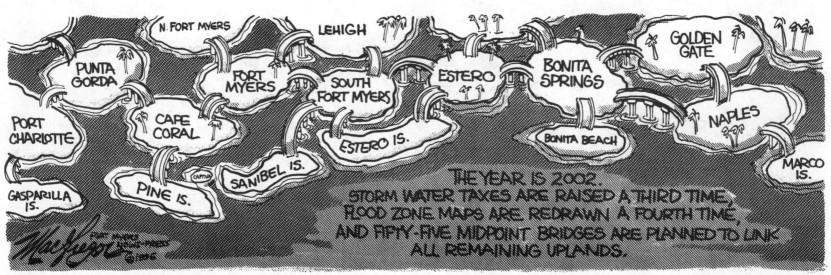

164

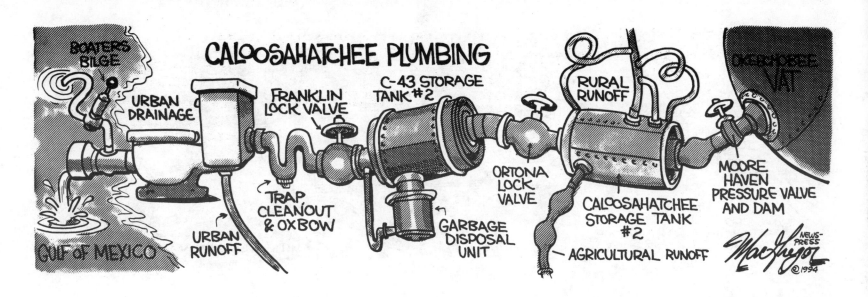

CALOOSAHATCHEE PLUMBING

BOATERS BILGE

URBAN DRAINAGE

FRANKLIN LOCK VALVE

C-43 STORAGE TANK #2

RURAL RUNOFF

OKEECHOBEE VAT

GULF of MEXICO

URBAN RUNOFF

TRAP CLEANOUT & OXBOW

ORTONA LOCK VALVE

GARBAGE DISPOSAL UNIT

CALOOSAHATCHEE STORAGE TANK #2

AGRICULTURAL RUNOFF

MOORE HAVEN PRESSURE VALVE AND DAM

NEWS-PRESS
© 1994

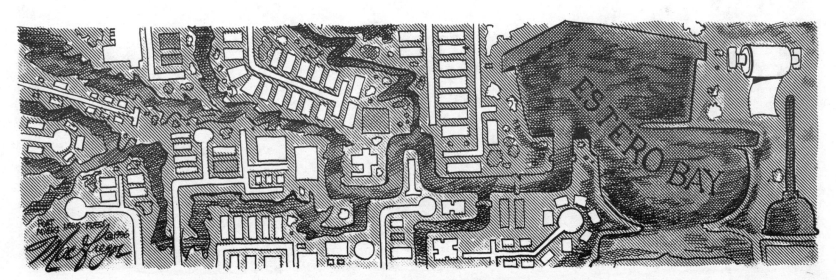

ESTERO BAY

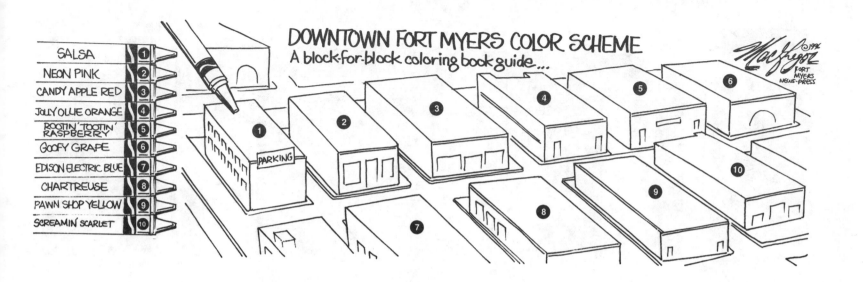

DOWNTOWN FORT MYERS COLOR SCHEME
A block-for-block coloring book guide...

SALSA	1
NEON PINK	2
CANDY APPLE RED	3
JOLLY OLLIE ORANGE	4
ROOTIN' TOOTIN' RASPBERRY	5
GOOFY GRAPE	6
EDISON ELECTRIC BLUE	7
CHARTREUSE	8
PAWN SHOP YELLOW	9
SCREAMIN' SCARLET	10

CITY of PALMS PARLOR GAMES ETC.
THIS WEEK'S EVENTS
TIDDLY WINKS CHAMPIONSHIP
CHARADES
PICK UP STICKS
MARBLE MANIA

Food Court
TODAY'S SPECIALS
TAFFY PULL
BOBBING FOR APPLES
COMING SOON ART LINK-LETTER

BIG TRIPLE FEATURE
MOVIES HEIDI, BAMBI, MARY POPPINS MOVIES
COMING SOON Pat Boone

CODE ENFORCEMENT POETRY READING

Playmate PLAYGROUND
NEXT WEEK
Lassie and Timmy do PET TRICKS

ARCADE
PIN THE TAIL ON THE DONKEY WOW!
WATCH PAINT DRY
A MUST SEE OZZIE & HARRIET AND DONNA REED RERUNS

FORT MYERS NEWS-PRESS
©1993

THAT'S LEGAL ENTERTAINMENT: Fort Myers, 2000 A.D.

169

MIDPOINT BRIDGE IS REALIGNED AND REDESIGNED

172

UNITED STATES of AMERICA?

CURRENT FLAG

FUTURE FLAG

TREE HUGGING STATES

NO TRESPASSING MY LAND STATES

IMMIGRANT-FRIENDLY STATES

GO BACK WHERE YOU CAME FROM STATES

PRO-LIFE STATES

ABORTION-LEGAL STATES

RIGHT TO DIE AT 65 MPH STATES

STATES THAT PROTECT GAY RIGHTS

HOMO-PHOBE STATES

WELFARE STATES

NON-WELFARE STATES

THESE PEOPLE ARE:

□ **A.** TERRIFIED OF THE HEADLESS HORSEMAN □ **B.** WITNESSING A CHAINSAW MASSACRE
□ **C.** AVOIDING A GRIZZLY BEAR ☑ **D.** WATCHING FORD, BUSH AND CLINTON PLAY GOLF

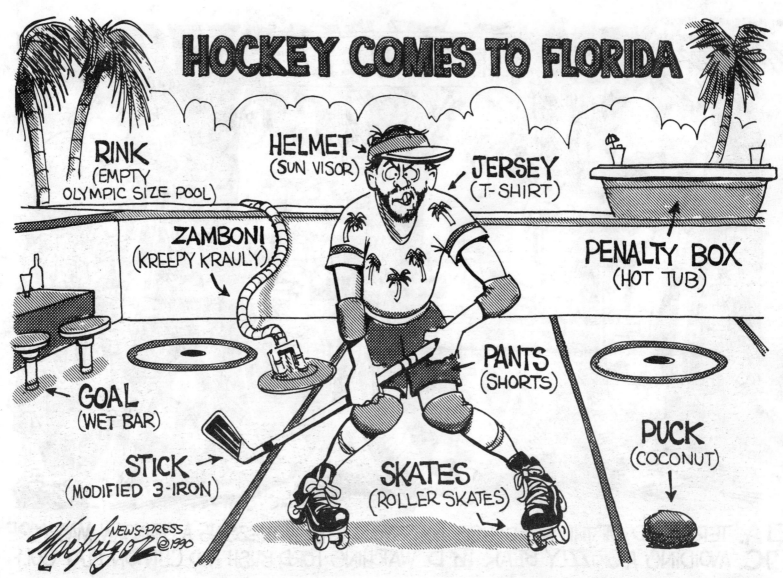

178

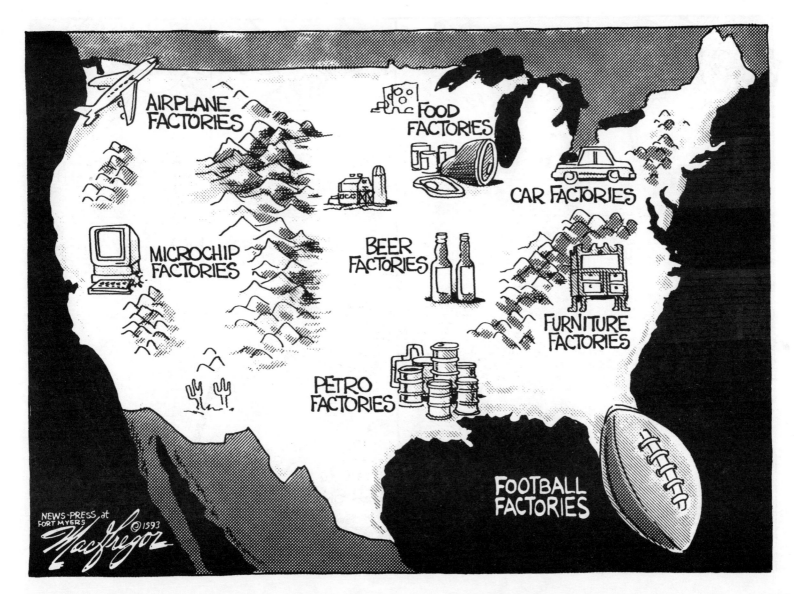

ON THE FIRST DAY GOD CREATED LIGHT

ON THE SECOND DAY HE BROUGHT FORTH WATER

ON THE THIRD DAY HE PLANTED GRASS

ON THE FOURTH DAY HE ADDED SUNSHINE TO MOW THE FIELD

ON THE FIFTH DAY HE CREATED MIGHTY GATORS

ON THE SIXTH DAY HE CREATED POWERFUL SEMINOLES

... ON THE SEVENTH DAY HE RESTED, GRABBED THE REMOTE CONTROL AND TOOK IN THE *BIG* GAME.

NFL MATCHUP

MATCH THE TEAM WITH ITS
HOME CITY OF THE FUTURE

SEATTLE

BALTIMORE

CLEVELAND

ST. LOUIS

LOS ANGELES

FANS

WHAT TO DO WITH OLYMPIC TERRORISTS

NEWS-PRESS at
FORT MYERS
© 1594
MacGregor

187

Last few conversation peaces...

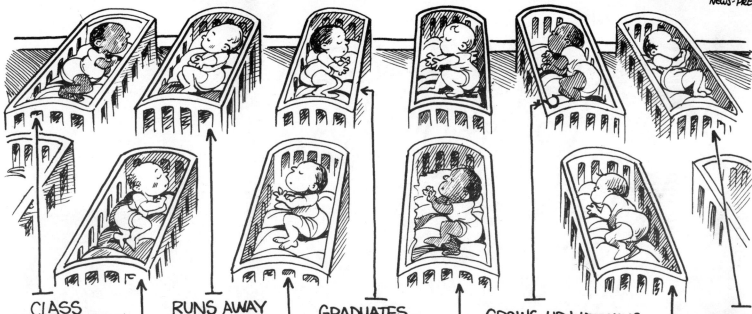

190

"Someday soon Santa...a cure if you can"